World Languages

Families in French

Daniel Nunn

Raintree is an imprint of Capstone Global Library Limited, a company incorporated in England and Wales having its registered office at 7 Pilgrim Street, London, EC4V 6LB – Registered company number: 6695582

To contact Raintree please phone 0845 6044371, fax + 44 (0) 1865 312263, or email: myorders@raintreepublishers.co.uk. Customers from outside the UK please telephone +44 1865 312262.

Edited by Daniel Nunn, Rebecca Rissman & Sian Smith
Designed by Joanna Hinton-Malivoire
Picture research by Tracy Cummins
Production by Victoria Fitzgerald
Originated by Capstone Global Library Ltd
Printed and bound in China by Leo Paper Products Ltd

ISBN 978 1 4062 5085 5
16 15 14 13 12
10 9 8 7 6 5 4 3 2 1

British Library Cataloguing in Publication Data
Nunn, Daniel.
Families in French: les families. – (World languages. Families)
1. French language–Vocabulary–Pictorial works–Juvenile literature. 2. Families–France–Terminology–Pictorial works–Juvenile literature.
I. Title II. Series
448.1-dc23

Acknowledgements
We would like to thank the following for permission to reproduce photographs: Shutterstock pp.4 (Catalin Petolea), 5 (optimarc), 5, 6 (Petrenko Andriy), 5, 7 (Tyler Olson), 5, 8 (Andrey Shadrin), 9 (Erika Cross), 10 (Alena Brozova), 5, 11 (Maxim Petrichuk), 12 (auremar), 13 (Mika Heittola), 5, 14, 15 (Alexander Raths), 5, 16 (Samuel Borges), 17 (Vitalii Nesterchuk), 18 (pat138241), 19 (Fotokostic), 20 (Cheryl Casey), 21 (spotmatik).

Cover photographs of two women and a man reproduced with permission of Shutterstock (Yuri Arcurs). Cover photograph of a girl reproduced with permission of istockphoto (© Sean Lockes). Back cover photograph of a girl reproduced with permission of Shutterstock (Erika Cross).

We would like to thank Séverine Ribierre for her invaluable help in the preparation of this book.

Every effort has been made to contact copyright holders of material reproduced in this book. Any omissions will be rectified in subsequent printings if notice is given to the publisher.

Contents

Salut! .4

Ma mère et mon père 6

Mon frère et ma soeur 8

Ma belle-mère et mon beau-père 10

Mon demi-frère et ma demi-soeur 12

Ma grand-mère et mon grand-père 14

Ma tante et mon oncle 16

Mes cousins 18

Mes amis 20

Dictionary 22

Index and notes 24

Salut!

Je m'appelle Daniel.

My name is Daniel.

Et voici ma famille.

And this is my family.

Ma mère et mon père

ma mère

Voici ma mère.

This is my mother.

mon père

Voici mon père.

This is my father.

Mon frère et ma soeur

mon frère

Voici mon frère.

This is my brother.

ma soeur

Voici ma soeur.

This is my sister.

Ma belle-mère et mon beau-père

ma belle-mère

Voici ma belle-mère.

This is my step-mother.

Voici mon beau-père.

This is my step-father.

Mon demi-frère et ma demi-soeur

mon demi-frère

Voici mon demi-frère.

This is my step-brother.

ma demi-soeur

Voici ma demi-soeur.

This is my step-sister.

Ma grand-mère et mon grand-père

ma grand-mère

Voici ma grand-mère.

This is my grandmother.

mon grand-père

Voici mon grand-père.

This is my grandfather.

Ma tante et mon oncle

ma tante

Voici ma tante.

This is my aunt.

mon oncle

Voici mon oncle.

This is my uncle.

Mes cousins

ma cousine

Voici mes cousins.

These are my cousins.

mon cousin

Mes amis

mon amie

Voici mes amis.

These are my friends.

mon ami

Dictionary

French word	How to say it	English word
ami	a-mee	friend (male)
amie	a-mee	friend (female)
amis	a-mee	friends
beau-père	bo-pair	step-father
belle-mère	bell-mair	step-mother
cousin	koo-zan	cousin (male)
cousine	koo-zeen	cousin (female)
cousins	koo-zan	cousins
demi-frère	de-mee-frair	step-brother
demi-soeur	de-mee-sir	step-sister
et	ay	and
famille	fa-mee-ya	family
frère	frair	brother
grand-mère	gron-mair	grandmother
grand-père	gron-pair	grandfather
je m'appelle	juh ma-pell	my name is

French word	How to say it	English word
ma	ma	my (female)
mère	mair	mother
mes	may / mez*	my (plural)
mon	mon	my (male)
oncle	on-kle	uncle
père	pair	father
salut	sa-loo	hi
soeur	sir	sister
tante	tont	aunt
voici	vwa-see	this is / these are

* 'Mes' is pronounced 'mez' when placed before a word beginning with a vowel.

See words in the "How to say it" columns for a rough guide to pronunciations.

Index

aunt 16

brother 8, 12

cousin 18, 19

friend 20, 21

grandparent 14, 15

parent 6, 7, 10, 11

sister 9, 13

uncle 17

Notes for parents and teachers

In French, nouns are either masculine or feminine. The word for 'my' changes accordingly – either 'mon' (masculine) or 'ma' (feminine). Sometimes nouns have different spellings too, which is why the word for 'cousin' can be spelled either 'cousin' (male) or 'cousine' (female).

On page 20 the masculine word 'mon' is used in the label 'mon amie' even though the word 'amie' is feminine. This is an exception, and occurs to avoid having the 'a' ending of 'ma' immediately alongside the 'a' sound at the start of 'amie'.